LIFE SKILLS
FOR KIDS

How to Cook, Clean, Make Friends, Handle
Emergencies, Set Goals, Make Good Decisions,
and Everything in Between

KAREN HARRIS

FREE BONUS

SCAN TO GET OUR NEXT BOOK FOR FREE!

TABLE OF CONTENTS

INTRODUCTION

There are two things that most kids and pre-teens wish they had: a driver's license and being old enough to do what they want so fewer people (parents excluded) can boss them around.

If this sounds familiar, you're on a big boat floating in a big ocean with a lot of other people about your own age. Trust me, I know.

Of course, you have other things on your mind, too, such as friends, video games, and movies. You may even start to think about romantic relationships (I had my first crush when I was eleven) or even your future education and what you want to be when you grow up.

I learned many of the lessons discussed here in school. I call them life hacks — important life skills. Life skills prepare you for, well, the rest of your life. They're lessons my parents taught me, such as how to handle conflict, manage time and prioritize responsibilities. There are also some practical day-to-day lessons, like how to run a dishwasher, do your laundry, and call 911 in the event of an emergency.

If you're intrigued, or you have questions about how to navigate life and its complexities, you're in the right place.

CHAPTER ONE:

UNDERSTANDING YOURSELF

SELF-CONTROL

Self-control is managing your behavior, especially how you react to people and situations around you. Here's an example. Say you're waiting in line to buy something at a store, and someone butts in line ahead of you. You have the right to tell them to go to the end of the line and wait like everyone else. (Chances are good you'll also get support from others waiting patiently in line with you.) Politely pointing this out to the offender is the right thing to do. However, if you get angry and raise your voice while pointing (pointedly) to the end of the line and jabbing your finger in that direction, your self-control just climbed out the window. Even though it's tempting to overreact, if your polite effort to convince the offender to go to the end of the line doesn't work, then you should find a store employee or manager to handle the situation for you. That's an example of practicing good self-control.

Self-control isn't always about emotions and feelings. It can also involve danger, peer pressure, or family values. For example, maybe your family taught you to share what you have with those who are less fortunate. If one of your friends forgot to pack their lunch, your first reaction might be you're sure they won't do that again after fighting hunger pains all afternoon. Besides, you want to eat your entire lunch because you're starving, and it sure looks good. However, you were taught good manners, *and* you sympathize with your friend's plight. Practicing good self-control, in this case, might be sharing half your lunch with your friend, so you each have something to eat to hold you over until you get your hands on a huge after-school snack.

Another example is if your friends encourage you to do something dangerous that you know is *not* okay. By practicing self-control instead, you think about the rules you've been taught and the potential consequences of your actions if you listen to your friends, not to mention possible injuries.

I'll give you a few tips that make building self-control easier.

Say no to temptation. If you're tempted to do something you know will get you in trouble, just say no. That's always better than getting in trouble with parents or teachers at school. Let's face it; temptation is tempting, but if you give yourself some time to think it over, you give self-control a chance to save the day (or at least save yourself from a lecture from your parents). Practicing self-control (instead of skipping school or not doing your homework, for example) goes a long way toward making you a smart kiddo and a wise adult in the making.

Set and follow priorities. You've probably heard this a few times at home and by now in school. Maybe there was a time you wanted to do something fun, but there was something less fun you were supposed to do — perhaps babysitting your little brother or raking leaves in the yard. You need to get your priorities straight now before you make a mistake. You may not know how to set priorities if you're still in grade school. (What is a priority, anyway?) Setting priorities can be hard at first, and you may need an adult to help you figure it out. So here's a quick down-and-dirty rule to help you figure it out: a priority is something you need to do to avoid getting in trouble for not doing it. Examples of priorities are doing your homework, cleaning the kitchen after dinner, studying for tomorrow's quiz, and babysitting your little brother. Knowing what's most important and deserves your immediate time and energy right away is what prioritizing is all about.

Forgive Yourself. There will be days when things don't go well. Maybe you forgot to do something, you made a bad choice, or you let someone down. Although you may feel bad, it's okay to cut yourself some slack. If your intentions were good, forgive yourself, then do what you can to fix whatever happened. You're only human, and many valuable life lessons stem from mistakes. Learn and move on.

LEARNING EFFECTIVE SKILLS

Below, you'll find a list of life skills you might need as a young person growing up fast.

Good hygiene. Hygiene is keeping yourself neat and clean, something that everyone needs to do. This includes bathing, combing your hair, brushing your teeth, keeping your hands clean, and wearing clean clothes every day. These are skills you'll use your entire life, and you've likely been doing them for years, so keep up the good work!

Organizational skills. Being organized means keeping your belongings in logical places where you can always find them, like clothes in a closet or a dresser. Keeping your room tidy allows you to easily find what you want and feel good about the space you live in. Maintaining organization is always smart, especially as life gets more complicated, as it will as you grow.

Money skills. Even as a kid, it's important to start learning about money and how to be responsible with it. Whenever you receive some money, for doing chores or on your birthday, get into the habit of saving some of it rather than spending it all. That's a simple habit that will have a lasting impact throughout your life. Having money in the bank is a great feeling; trust me on that.

There are many other skills to explore as we progress, but these are basic ones everyone needs to know to get off to a good start in life.

CHAPTER TWO:

LEARN FROM FAILURE

Wouldn't it be great if nothing ever went wrong in life and everything was utopian (perfect)? Sadly, life isn't typically like that. However, a very important thing to understand is that some of the best lessons people learn in life come from their failures. Failure lessons arrive in many forms, and everyone bumps into failure at least a few times growing up. That's one thing we all have in common. (Again, trust me on that.) A solid gold silver lining to failure is that it's one of the most powerful ways to learn, as most of us discover one way or another.

Most people find failure painful, daunting, difficult, and/or dispiriting. Failure can make you question yourself, your abilities, and even your worth. This happens because we misunderstand it. We think of failure as something to be avoided at all costs.

You might think you're the only one who fails, and everyone else slides into home plate with towering success *every single time*. You might think you should just give up (a big mistake, by the way). The best way to handle failure is by embracing it (not intuitive, I know), but failure is inevitable; no one avoids it!

If you look at failure as a learning opportunity, you're automatically on the right track. Take the story of Thomas Edison, inventor of the light bulb. Edison was considered a failure; he was fired from two jobs for being "nonproductive." He was the failed inventor of the electric pen, tinfoil phonograph, a talking doll, an ore mill, a kinetoscope (early motion picture device), and of course, the light bulb. Edison made 1,000 failed attempts at the light bulb (some say 10,000 failed attempts). Today he is known as the *genius* who invented the light bulb none of us could get along without. Remember that the next time you're kicking yourself for failing at something.

Before Edison's success, there were many failed projects made by many people, and each one was necessary to finally bring electricity to every home. Imagine what life must have been like for early experimenters Alessandro Volta and Michael

Faraday, who tried and failed at various projects related to electricity, sometimes burning up their labs and having to start over writing formulas and spending resources only to discover an invention totally by accident. Instead of giving up, their toil, failure, and eventual luck ultimately led to the invention of electricity and changed the course of life on Earth.

People often hide their failures as something shameful, preferring to discuss the things they're proud of. But don't forget Edison's many failed attempts to reach one singular success.

The Oxford Dictionary defines failure as "the negligence or omission of expected or required action." This basically means that failure is an unmet expectation or something that didn't happen the way you thought it would. That's not so awful, is it?

Failure is just an opportunity to do something again, only better. Failure, while often uncomfortable, is easier to navigate the more life experience you have. The more things you try and fail at, the more you'll learn about yourself and how to rebound after a setback. Those lessons will come in handy the next time you face a challenge.

People make failure worse than it needs to be because they worry what others will think, or they engage in negative self-talk, meaning they tell themselves bad things like they're no good, not smart enough, or are unworthy. That kind of baloney makes you feel terrible. Instead, tell yourself things you would say to a friend in the same situation. "That was a great idea! I'm sure you'll do better next time."

This brings us to the place of accepting our failures and using them to become better, stronger people. Failure is an uncomfortable place to be, and the thought of accepting it is hard for the mind to grasp. This is only natural; we tend to avoid things that don't feel good.

Here are some important steps to override that basic urge to treat failure as the enemy.

DON'T GET UPSET!

Acknowledge failure. You can admit that your outcome is not the one you wanted. This puts you in the right frame of mind for the next step. It opens you to feel the pain you would have avoided if you ignored the outcome.

Acknowledge your feelings: I think this step is the most difficult one. It requires you to examine and acknowledge the disappointment, pain, anger, confusion, or sadness. You need to ask questions like, "What did I do wrong?" which could help you have a better outcome in the future.

Talk to a friend, family member, or trusted adult. This can be an important part of learning from failure. If you keep those feelings inside, you may not examine everything that happened and learn from it. Often, talking through challenges with someone else can shed new light on the situation, which is necessary for you to learn and move forward successfully.

SEE THE OPPORTUNITY
IN FAILURE

Toddlers approach potential failure with curiosity. They fall and get back up, walking and bumping into things with unsteady gait, trying to pronounce words and getting them wrong but squealing with glee when they get it right. If only we could all approach challenges and learning with such freedom and a complete lack of self-consciousness!

Regaining enthusiasm for learning after a failure is a valuable skill. Lessons to learn from failure include:

Failing forward. Failing is an opportunity to do something again and do it better. This is called failing forward—every mistake is a forward opportunity to do it better when you do it again. Failure gives you a real opportunity to practice, prepare, and train. Failure is a learning opportunity and a necessary step toward success.

Failure may reveal better opportunities. Netflix is a company that never intended to stream movies. Its original mission was accessible entertainment, and its first strategy was sending DVDs in the mail. As technology advanced, people wanted to either stream movies at home or use familiar brick-and-mortar movie rental stores. While solid, the plan didn't bring about the success Netflix imagined, which presented the "opportunity" to go back to the drawing board. Its "failure" and subsequent dream led the company to where it is today. Sometimes when you fail at something, it's beneficial to find different and better ways to do what you originally set out to do.

Failure teaches growth. Failure is a test of character. It tests your maturity and how you handle life's disappointments. Taking failure in stride and finding healthy ways to cope with disappointment can make the difference between a well-adjusted future adult or an adult who sidesteps the effort.

Failure can teach better communication. Express honest feelings about your failure. Letting yourself be vulnerable when talking to parents and friends is a sign that you're emotionally mature rather than emotionally vulnerable or weak.

Although no one likes failure, over time, it helps you build confidence, self-esteem, and the ability to successfully tackle whatever comes your way.

CHAPTER THREE:
GOOD DECISION MAKING

Decision-making is the act of making choices—hopefully, wise ones. Knowing how to make good decisions is a valuable life skill that affects you, your family and friends, and the world around you every day.

People make decisions almost every moment of the day, including what to eat, what to wear, who to hang out with, and who to avoid. When you're very young, adults make all your decisions because they're older and wiser, and along the way, they learned from their own life experiences and from their parents before them.

Some decisions are easy; they're either right or wrong based on what you were taught as a child. You know not to steal, not to cheat, not to hit people, and to be polite, honest, and kind. In those straightforward situations, correct decisions yield good results, while wrong decisions lead to not-so-good results.

Wrong decisions can lead to dangerous situations, and right decisions to generally good outcomes But other times, right and wrong aren't so obvious. Sometimes you have more than one option for how to handle a situation, not just choice one or choice two. It may be impossible to know what the best choice is. This is where good decision-making comes in.

There are many ways to approach complicated decisions, and you can always request the help of a trusted friend or adult. Following are a few choices to make when you don't know what to do.

MAKE NO CHOICE

Simply choose not to decide. This allows someone else to make the decision. This is okay if the decision to be made isn't a major one. If your dad asks, "What do you want for dinner?" and you don't have a preference, you can say, "Anything is fine. You decide." Leaving decisions like this to others is often just fine.

But when you have a bigger, more important decision to make, you want to have an active say in the matter. Remember that every time you make a decision, it's easier to make the next one. You can still seek the opinion of people like your parents, teachers, siblings, or coaches. But once you've had time to think it over, you can make the decision on your own.

MAKING CHOICES WITHOUT THINKING

Not all decisions take a lot of time to make. Sometimes you won't have a preference, and you let someone else make the decision, like what to have for dinner. Other times you know your answer right away, and you don't need much time to think it through. This is often true for small things.

Your brother may ask, "Do you want to wear a red shirt or a green shirt today?" and you immediately answer, "Red!" No one has to think twice about that one; it's a small decision.

For more important decisions, it's best to take time to consider every option. Make sure you understand the situation, every possible outcome and that everyone involved has had time to think it through.

When faced with an important decision, take your time to think. Don't rush to a decision before you're ready. If you're used to making quick decisions without thinking, at least know that when a big one comes along, you need to take time to consider it carefully.

THOUGHTFUL DECISION-MAKING

Thoughtful decision-making means considering all sides of the issue at hand. You may want to consider the opinions of others you trust; they may have viewpoints you didn't think about. This is where seeking help from other knowledgeable people can help a lot.

The following are steps to follow when considering a decision.

Identify the issue. Make sure the issue is clearly understood before you make a decision.

Gather relevant information. Do research if necessary, and talk to those who can offer good advice to learn more about the issue. Make a point of hearing how others involved feel and take their feelings into account.

List possible solutions. Think carefully, and don't rush to just finish and get it over with. When you have several possible solutions, choose the one that best suits your needs.

Learning Self-Control. This is the process of keeping yourself in check, especially when it comes to considering others. Resist the urge to act without thinking carefully about a decision. There are many ways to practice self-control, and you probably do this all the time, whether you realize it or not. You practice self-control when you sit still in class, use good table manners when eating, and sit quietly in church.

Simple, common examples of good self-control that lead to good decision-making are:

- Being quiet when others are speaking.
- Using polite manners. Different cultures have different rules. Respect what you've been taught, as well as good manners and practices from other cultures.
- Examples of poor decision-making or lack of self-control:
- Interrupting others
- Taking things without permission
- Lack of tolerance or patience

In summary, carefully consider all factors and sides when you have a decision to make. Don't rush to decide, and take time to seek the advice of those you respect. If you take your time to discuss, think, and research until you are satisfied, you will likely make a wise, thoughtful decision.

CHAPTER FOUR:

THE RIGHT ATTITUDE FOR SUCCESS

No single definition of *success* applies to everyone. As you get older, you will decide what success means to you. What do you want your life to look like? What's most important to you? Regardless of how you define success, having a positive attitude will help you to achieve your goals.

Whatever your goal is, it won't just drop from the sky into your lap one day. You'll have to set your goal and work to achieve it. The most important thing to be aware of is your attitude. Being optimistic and hopeful will help you achieve your goals.

STAYING POSITIVE

Being positive is a way of thinking and acting that influences your progress toward your career/life goal.

Staying positive includes:

Focusing on the good things. Studies have shown that people who look at the positive side of life and maintain hopeful attitudes are happier and healthier than people who are pessimistic. Some people naturally embody positivity. In fact, I have a friend, Jon, who's like a ray of sunshine wherever he goes. He is perennially happy and cheerful, whistling and smiling as he goes about his day. He has more friends than he can count, and everyone wants to be around him. Some of this is genetics, but part is just Jon's general attitude. He *chooses* to be happy; it's an active choice on his part. He's always been that way.

Maintain your favorite activities. Do the things you love to stay in a positive mindset. Whatever your passions are, dancing, singing in a choir, listening to great music, or reading the great American novel, stay active in all of them to maintain your happiness and balance.

Avoid comparisons with others. It's easy to compare yourself to other people; we do it all the time. However, comparisons are rarely helpful for a number of reasons. No one else's situation is exactly like yours, and comparing your blueberry self to your zucchini friend is like comparing apples and bananas — they just won't match up, and they aren't supposed to! Also, the more time you spend fretting about what others do or say, the less time you have to spend on the things you love.

Find your passion. This part is fun! Pay attention to what catches your eye and holds your interest. Pursue it and do the things that make you happy. Sometimes we get carried away pleasing others, doing things we don't really enjoy. For example, maybe you joined the soccer team because your friend is on the team, or you still take piano lessons because you know your mom wants you to, even though your heart's not in it anymore. There are times you have an obligation to see a responsibility through to completion, so you keep your word and do it (congratulations on your sterling character!), but balance what you *have* to do with what you *love* to do. Find the things that bring you joy and feed your soul on a regular basis.

Empathy. This is the ability to understand the emotions of another's situation and feelings. It helps you relate to others and makes you the type of warm, caring, well-rounded person others want to be around.

Set realistic expectations. Don't get carried away when you set goals for yourself. You might be so inspired by the achievements of others that you end up taking on more than you can handle. When you set a goal for yourself, make sure they're achievable and realistic based on your schedule and level of interest. Maybe you're inspired by a world-class surfer you've seen online, and you want to be a surfer, too. That's great, but if you live in the middle of a desert or in Canada, you'll find it difficult to do much surfing, except on vacations to California or Hawaii. That means your surfing goal might not be a realistic one at the present time. It doesn't mean you need to give up on that goal, but maybe you begin by setting goals to read about surfing, watch tutorials about surfing, and learn about the fitness goals you should pursue now to get ready for a surfing competition in the future. Don't pressure yourself and work at your own pace but stay active and interested.

GOAL SETTING

Follow the five Ws when setting goals. These are simple rules that go a long way in helping you achieve goals. The Ws are why, what, when, write, and work.

Why did you set those goals? Why do you want to do this? Don't skip setting goals; they are necessary and important.

What do you aim to achieve by setting these goals? Will they serve as stepping stones to other achievements later in life?

When do you hope to achieve your goals? Identifying deadlines to match your goals make achievement more likely. Set a start date, then set milestones you hope to reach along the way to your goal. Finally, set a deadline for the final goal.

Milestones help you achieve your goal faster, with opportunities to celebrate successes along the way. For example, if your goal is to learn a complicated new dance, just saying, "I want to learn the dance," is a big goal. Break it down into milestones with smaller achievable chunks you can focus on, celebrating accomplishments each time you finish one. Altogether, they will lead to your goal of mastering the entire dance.

Write down the goals you hope to achieve at the end of the whole program. Do not forget to put down the time frame you have chosen to work with, your start date and finish date, and your milestones and final deadline.

Start working toward your written goals. Focus on the ones to achieve first, then continue with the others. When you achieve them, they will be morale boosters to help you reach the ultimate goal.

Don't take shortcuts! Working hard for what you want really makes it all the more satisfying in the end.

CHAPTER FIVE:
COMMUNICATION

Knowing how to communicate effectively is an essential life skill. Babies communicate by crying, but from the age of two up, most people communicate by talking. You communicate best when you use words effectively.

Exercise Self-Control

When you have something to say, others listen best when you speak in a "room temperature" tone of voice. If you have a brilliant idea, no one will listen if you shout, or if they do, they won't take you seriously.

Avoid Tantrums

If you stamp your foot on the ground, shout at the top of the staircase, and refuse to eat, you will get your parents' attention, but everyone else will walk out the door. Tantrums are a bad habit; if you simply must have them, please do so in a padded room.

Speak Respectfully

When you speak, be mindful of other people's feelings and sensibilities. Do not use offensive language, and don't assume that other people feel the same way you do about politics and other sensitive subjects.

Active Listening

Listening actively to others during a conversation will give you insight into their beliefs and opinions. Active listening also allows you to have constructive conversations on safe topics (please).

Apologize When You Need To

When you do or say something wrong, apologize without delay. When you're wrong, don't be bull-headed and pretend everything is alright; that will likely lead to hard feelings. Once you make amends, chances are those around you will quickly let bygones be bygones.

Be Respectful of the Opinions of Others

Never make fun of someone else's opinions. They have the right to free speech, just like you do. A respectful exchange of opinions often leads to interesting and lively conversations.

Learning to Listen Actively

If you listen to others, they will listen to you, too.

Pay attention to the speaker. Be quiet, and you might learn something. Use attentive body language.

Don't interrupt, and wait your turn if you have something to say. Put your own thoughts aside or write them down. At the end of the speech, or when it is your turn to speak, politely make your comments.

Take Criticism Constructively

Constructive criticism is meant to show you what you've done well and how you can continue to improve. Despite these good intentions, constructive criticism can still be hard to accept, and sometimes feelings get hurt (even though this is not intended). It's best to take it in good faith and use it as a chance to correct mistakes and strive to improve in the future.

Dealing with constructive criticism takes maturity in areas of self-control and concentration.

- Listen carefully to what you're told.
- Do not get angry or ignore the source of criticism. Note the points made, and don't interrupt to defend yourself.
- Show appreciation and thank the source of the criticism for looking at your work or idea and ask for advice.
- Ask questions if you have them, and promise to take their advice seriously. Take corrective action as needed.

CHAPTER SIX:
KEEPING YOUR COOL IN AN EMERGENCY

The Cambridge Dictionary defines an emergency as something dangerous or serious, such as an accident that happens unexpectedly and needs fast action to avoid harmful results.

If you ever encounter or witness a situation like this, it's important to remain calm and focused so you can think clearly. Stay composed and follow procedures for handling emergencies.

Your parents, guardians, and teachers are the best source of information on handling emergencies since their guidance will be specific to your house or town. Below I list general suggestions to keep in mind, but be sure to discuss this in more detail with the trusted adults in your life.

Take deep breaths and remind yourself to stay calm.

Reach out for help. Call 911 first and then other adults who need to know.

Stay away from impending danger and inform those around you about the situation if they need to know.

It's important to know about emergency preparedness before an emergency happens. The tips discussed below will help you in an emergency.

Know how to use a cell phone and dial the universal emergency number: 911.

Memorize your parents' phone numbers and always have them saved in your own phone.

HOW TO CALL 911

- Dial 911 on the phone. No other numbers are required.
- Tell the operator over the phone that there is an emergency.
- Tell them your name, phone number, and where you are to the best of your ability. They may ask for your home address.
- They will ask you about the nature of the emergency, what happened, and whether there are injuries in need of medical

attention, along with other required information.

- Answer all questions to the best of your ability. This information helps dispatch first responders and equipment necessary to assist the situation

- The operator may give you instructions over the phone. Follow those instructions exactly and ask clarifying questions if necessary.

- Do not disconnect the call. Listen to everything the operator tells you. The 911 operator will disconnect the call when they have all the information they need.

- Wait for help to come. If anyone is injured, do not attempt to help them unless given instructions by 911 personnel or first responders.

HOW TO RELAY INFORMATION

In an emergency, the primary way of passing information to others is over the phone. Following are ways to effectively relay important, often time-sensitive, information.

First, don't panic and speak calmly. In most cases, the person who answers your call will be trained in communicating with people dealing with unexpected emergencies. That person is used to emergencies and will help you communicate effectively.

Do your best to give clear descriptions. You will be asked questions to help the other party (let's say it's the 911 dispatcher) understand the situation and what kind of help is needed (ambulance, fire truck, police, etc.).

YOUR PERSONAL INFORMATION

You will be asked for information that authorities may need to contact you for more details. Following are examples of information you may be asked for:

Your full name.

The location of the emergency (described as accurately as you can using landmarks, street names, or any other identifying information you can provide).

Your home address.

Your cell phone number.

Names and phone numbers of your parents or guardians. This may include their workplace information.

CHAPTER SEVEN:
CHORES MAKE LIFE EASIER

As part of a family, you are an important part of household activities, so doing your part in daily and weekly chores is normal. Each family member is responsible for doing their fair share.

Chores help keep your home clean and comfortable. They also teach you about responsibility, which is something that will always be part of life. You'll also learn about what it takes to keep a household running smoothly, and you'll become familiar with the great feeling of a job well done.

Not every chore is pleasant to take care of, but it makes life more pleasant when it's finished. This is a bit like bathing yourself regularly — it may not be your favorite thing to do, but it sure beats the alternative! So, resolve to make peace with your chores. One way or another, they need to be done, or one morning you may find yourself eating breakfast from a greasy, crusty plate because last night's dinner dishes weren't washed.

CHORES ARE LEARNING OPPORTUNITIES

If your mom asks you to do the laundry one Saturday, you might learn a lot about cleaning and maintaining clothing. If you toss your new wool sweater in with the bath towels, you might learn an expensive lesson about ruining a $75 sweater! Your mom might give you a stern but valuable lecture on the proper way to launder (and preserve) that wool sweater. Chances are you'll remember that lesson for the rest of your life, which will likely encompass the best way to safely clean most items in your wardrobe.

The skills you acquire by doing chores include:

- Problem solving
- Following written instructions
- Independent thinking
- Self-reliance
- Time management
- Prioritizing tasks

- Learning new skills
- Getting along with others
- Independence and maturity

Unexpected problems may arise when you're working around the house, like the kitchen sink clogging while the dishwasher runs. When you figure out the problem behind the malfunction (perhaps with the help of your parents), you will have learned something new that you will probably remember for a long time.

PRACTICING INDEPENDENCE

There are several definitions of independence. You may think of independence in terms of freedom from being ruled or controlled by others. Here, independence means being able to work on your own.

You're still a long way from living on your own and fully supporting yourself. Still, it's not too early to prepare yourself for the future. Having said that, these are the skills you should acquire to help you become independent.

- Saving money
- Dressing for the weather or an event
- Good personal hygiene
- Problem solving
- Time management
- Prioritizing tasks
- Goal setting

The many ways in which you can practice **personal hygiene** include bathing daily, brushing your teeth two or three times a day, wearing clean clothes, washing your hands before eating, keeping your nails clean and trimmed, and keeping your immediate living environment clean.

Setting goals is not just limited to your academic work, although it's an excellent way to ensure that your schoolwork gets done well and on time. You can set a goal to make the basketball team or become an award-winning journalist. You may want to reach a goal of $1,000 in your savings account, or you may just want to make a masterful Baked Alaska for a special occasion. Go for it!

Setting milestones breaks down long-term goals into smaller, easily achievable tasks to be worked on step by step. If the goal is having a clean bedroom, tackling it all at once might leave you wiped out and perhaps more disorganized. Instead, start with making your bed, then pick up your dirty clothes, straighten your bookshelf and use the feather duster, and in no time, you'll have a clean bedroom. And lucky you, you just made a plan to tackle a big job in small, easily digestible steps. This process will eventually create a habit that's easy to stay on top of.

Goals aren't always achieved immediately, and big jobs take time to accomplish. That's why **patience** is a virtue. If you practice patience, ask for help when needed, and don't give up, you'll be proud of yourself when the job is finished. Looks like you've got this!

CHAPTER EIGHT:

TIME MANAGEMENT

Time management is the ability to spend your time in a productive manner. Despite all the hours in a day, if your time is not used well, it will always feel like not enough.

How good are you at organizing your time, so you get the important things done properly? When you start to do something, do you focus all your attention on it and get it finished? If any of these are things you struggle with, it's time to start working on your time management skills!

LEARNING TO PRIORITIZE

Prioritizing means doing important work before doing less important work. It doesn't mean that what needs to be done is unimportant; it means that something undesirable could happen if the *more* important things don't get done first. Here's a simple example. If you don't stop to get milk on Monday afternoon, you can't have milk on your cereal Tuesday morning. Buying milk on Monday was *prioritized* so that milk is available for breakfast Tuesday morning.

As you build the discipline to finish your responsibilities on time, you will find there's more time left over for other things, like hobbies with friends and family.

DEVELOPING A ROUTINE

A routine is a pattern you follow to achieve a goal. Routines are things you do every day or on a regular basis. For instance, every morning when you wake up, you get dressed, eat breakfast, brush your teeth, and go to school. That's your morning *weekday* routine. You may have a Saturday routine that involves chores around the house and playtime, while your Sunday routine may involve going to church and having dinner with relatives.

Routines are nice because they incorporate habits that help you get things done. However, they shouldn't be so rigid that there's no room to fit in other important things. Occasionally you may need to have a dental appointment, so arrangements might be made for you to leave school 30 minutes before classes are dismissed to get to your appointment on time.

Another routine may be doing your homework right after dinner. The nice thing about this is that time is set aside to get your homework done and still leave free time for you afterward.

Routines utilize time management and priorities so that goals are accomplished, making life a little easier and less stressful.

Reward yourself for sticking to your routines. Creating a routine and staying with it is not easy; hence the need to reward yourself for a job well done. For example, if your goal is to finish your assignments every day just before your parents get home, reward yourself with some free time outside afterward.

CHAPTER NINE:

FINANCIAL AWARENESS

If the goal is to build wealth for the future (real meaning: having a lot of money when you grow up), and to live well as an adult, learning about money is a skill you should know about *now!*

As a child, my fascination with money began when I developed an obsession with music. I loved Yanni and the Backstreet Boys, but I really didn't care what music I got — I just wanted to own a huge collection. I asked my parents for money whenever my allowance ran out, and my dad always asked me what I'd do to earn it because, as he put it, he wasn't a bank.

My mind was blown; all along, I thought my dad was rich! I knew enough from seeing my friends' houses to know we didn't have a pool in our house for a reason but having him acknowledge the limit of his resources was a rude awakening that really made me think.

I thought about all the money I'd seen my parents spend, and I imagined what it would be like if my dad had saved every penny he ever made; then, I added in every penny my mom ever made. We sure would have been rich then!

That calculation, and the urge to devise ways to earn my own money, propelled me into the world of financial literacy (which means understanding money in plain English).

A lot of people—especially on the Internet—have ideas and opinions about what kids should be allowed to see or do. When the topic of financial literacy (understanding money) comes up, people say things like, "Why burden him with this now?" or "Let her be a child before she grows up!"

But this ignores the fact that it's a disservice to young people not to teach them what they need to know about money from an early age. Even though I started educating myself about money early, and my mom and dad were the teachers who helped me learn how to save, as well as the concept of saving and earning compound interest, there are still a lot of things I wish I'd known before I started saving and investing.

Let's talk about the ways you can earn money and spend it wisely. We will also talk about how your money can get away from you. Sometimes the need to satisfy an impulse might make you do things that are not acceptable or safe just to earn money. This is not right.

EARNING MONEY

It is never too early to start earning money and practicing good money habits. Remember, the more you practice something, the better you'll get. Starting small now will help you build strong money skills later.

But how to make money? Well, it could be as easy as letting people in your neighborhood know you'll cut the grass or weed the vegetable garden. You can offer to take a child to a nearby park. Perhaps the lady down the road needs someone to feed her cat and water her plants when she goes to visit her granddaughter. Ask a trusted adult and neighbors you already know for help coming up with money-making ideas. More than likely, they can help you find suitable work.

Here are some great ways to make money I took advantage of when I was a student. These may or may not apply to you and your neighborhood, or they might need revamping before they can be profitable for you.

- Do chores for your parents and neighbors
- Dog walking
- Run errands for neighbors
- Tutor classmates on difficult topics
- Care for pets when their owners go on vacation

SAVING MONEY

The next step on this journey is saving money. Knowing how to make money without knowing how to hold onto the money you have defeats the whole purpose of earning it in the first place. What's the point, then, if you only have it long enough to spend all of it and end up right where you started?

Here are a couple of tips you need to acquire to make and keep your money.

Exercise restraint. This is important! Of course, you can spend some of the money you earn; just don't let it burn a hole in your pocket. (You'll not only have a sore leg, but your money will be gone, and you'll have to throw your pants away, too.) When spending, do so wisely, keeping a portion of your earnings for another time and *always* putting some in your savings account—you'll never be sorry you did. This is called delayed gratification; it means you want something, but you're willing to wait for a time when you can better afford it without breaking the bank.

Budget wisely. Always have a plan for your money. If you don't have a plan, your money will definitely find a way to get away from you. Decide what's important to you when it comes to money, and make a plan to ensure you save for what you really want or need.

Be disciplined: Learning how to do something consistently, even when no one's watching, is an excellent example of self-discipline. Make your financial decisions and stick to them, even when you really want that new gizmo all your friends have. It's like building muscle; you get better at it the longer you practice.

Spend wisely. Spending without forethought is a bad habit. There are certain things one should know before spending money on anything. The steps discussed below will help you learn to spend money wisely.

Ask your parents for advice. Growing up, I always wondered why we bought generic cornflakes at the grocery store instead of Kelloggs. Or why did we buy from another store twenty minutes away instead of from the mall that was a ten-minute walk down our street? When my parents explained that sometimes it made sense to drive farther to get a better price on household goods, that was a big budget lesson I didn't know I needed.

Use discount stores or coupons. Making a purchase and getting a good price is a great feeling. The first time I bought something from the sales rack at Target and saved money, I was thrilled, and I craved that feeling again. I always found ways to save on the things I wanted. This is a great quality to have when you're learning how to make money and keep it.

CHAPTER TEN:
OPERATING APPLIANCES

I know, I know. I see you rolling your eyes. You're thinking, "But I don't need to know that stuff! My parents take care of it."

You may be right for now, but since most of this book is about equipping you for the future, and you will *definitely* need this information when you live independently, pay attention. We live in an increasingly complex world, and things are getting easier, so settle down and keep reading.

Knowing how to operate basic home appliances is a key skill you need, even if you don't use it often. Every skill you acquire will definitely be used at least a few times in the course of your life (trust me once again). I know this because my brother once got a summer job simply because he knew how to put a tabletop appliance back together in a pinch.

First, it was my dad's Grundig Satellite 650 radio, then my mom's new microwave door that wouldn't close just right anymore. One morning we woke up, and the fridge door fell apart when I did nothing more than look at it. I think my dad secretly enjoyed fixing things with my brother in tow and forcing him to learn, too.

In college, my brother was at a diner with some friends when the food processor exploded. The smoke and the noise spooked the customers and some of the staff. My brother swung over the counter like he worked there and fixed it for them. The manager immediately offered him a summer job that he kept until he graduated. Who says fix-it skills don't come in handy?

For the rest of this chapter, we'll look at the common kitchen appliances you should know how to use, that is, if you tend to get hungry on a regular basis.

HOW TO USE A WASHING MACHINE

Knowing how to wash your clothes at home is important! Trust me. While it may look like dumping your clothes in the machine and pressing a few buttons, it's a little more complicated than that.

You need to know the following, so your clothes come out clean and undamaged.

Type of material: Some clothes need a gentle wash, as opposed to vigorous agitation and spinning. Knowing this is important, as some machines have options for different kinds of fabric. All you have to do is follow the label instructions.

Temperature: Learn the right temperature for each type of fabric (knits, permanent press, etc.) You don't want your clothes shrinking or stretching in the wash.

Detergent: Adding the right type of detergent might seem trivial, and you might be tempted to just pour in any old soap and start tumbling, but this could ruin your clothes. Consult the fabric labels on each item or on the Internet for the correct amount of detergent and water temperature to use before you start.

Type of machine: Using a top loader is a little easier than a front loader, and using each properly will prolong the life of your machine, as well as your clothes.

HOW TO OPERATE THE DISHWASHER

This used to be my least favorite chore. My dad had a rule: whoever helped make the meal didn't have to do the dishes, and whoever finished eating last got stuck loading the dishwasher.

A big believer in self-sufficiency, my dad was never very quick to offer help when we worked on something difficult. He wanted us to try fixing things first, making our own mistakes, before he offered his help. So, when I learned to use the dishwasher, I spent a whole day reading the instruction manual from the manufacturer's site on the Internet before I got a clean load. I was so proud of myself!

To start out, different dishwashers have different settings, and if you can read and follow instructions, you might be able to wing it on your first try. If not, a YouTube video will come in handy.

Here are a few helpful tips for using any kind of dishwasher.

Before loading the washer, scrape and rinse dirty plates in the sink to remove pieces of food. This will keep your drain open. (Cleaning the drain is a lot messier than doing the dishes, I assure you.)

Place the dirty plates in the plate slots and don't block the water sprayers, which is guaranteed to result in dirty dishes.

After the dirty plates are loaded, **close and lock the door** and choose the washing and/or drying method of your choice. Which options you choose (heated dry cycle or extra hot wash) will depend on what you've loaded into the machine (dishes vs. pots and pans) and how dirty they are.

Do not interrupt the machine during the cycle. A typical washing cycle lasts about an hour.

OPERATING THE STOVE AND MICROWAVE

Eating is a survival skill *and* a life skill. Learning to use the most common cooking appliances always comes in handy no matter what you do in the future.

The first thing to learn about cooking appliances is safety first. Always use extreme caution around heat and fire, so you don't burn yourself or your food.

Microwaves are used to cook, bake, defrost, and heat your food. There are simple, straightforward ways to use a microwave and get efficient results. Always familiarize yourself with the manual that comes with your microwave. This goes a long way toward cooking food successfully the way you want it without running into problems.

Put the food in a microwave-safe container. That means no metal and nothing that could melt (like some plastics). It's extremely dangerous to put any type of metal, including aluminum foil, in the microwave. This causes sparking and possible fire.

Use a dish, paper towel, or wax paper to cover the food you're going to cook in the microwave, especially if it's something like sauce or soup that could splatter. (Splatters can make a big mess in the microwave. Trust me on this.)

Set a timer for the duration you want your food to cook. Use the timer available on your model to set the cooking time.

If you wish to stop or pause the cooking process before it's complete, use the buttons on the machine or just open the door. Otherwise, allow the food to heat.

Using a **stove** is easy as long as you follow the instruction manual carefully. Your manual will give you directions about using the stove as well as the oven. The burners on your stove may be gas, electric, or flat-top glass.

Keep away flammable material or long hair away from the stove burners at all times. Roll your sleeves up, and if you have long hair, tie it back securely. (The normal oils in your hair are highly flammable, so make sure your hair is kept away from the stove.)

If your home has a gas stove, ask an adult for help to turn it on and show you how to use it. There are special safety precautions for gas stoves in particular, so you'll need guidance and supervision while learning this.

If you have an electric stove, it will be a bit easier to learn how to use it. You'll need to understand how the knobs work and what the different settings mean. This prevents you from burning food or risking a fire.

Turn off the stove after every use. Do not leave it on while engaging in other activities, and *do not* use it to warm the house when it's cold outside. This is a serious fire risk.

USING THE VACUUM CLEANER

Vacuum cleaners are household appliances that lift dirt, dust, and small items off floors, furniture, and draperies. Vacuum cleaners are typically upright or canister style. Some vacuums have bags inside the housing that catch and trap the dirt pulled up. If your vacuum cleaner has a disposable bag rather than a reusable canister, you may need adult assistance when changing the bag for the first time. Some vacuums are bagless, which saves money buying bags. Bagless vacuums empty the dirt into a reusable container that is later emptied into your household trash. Machines of all types with full bags or canisters don't clean as well as empty ones.

Most models adjust for floor height, where hardwood or vinyl flooring is the lowest setting, and carpet settings vary based on the length of the pile.

Remove small objects that might get pulled into the suction path. Objects like toys, clothes, shoelaces, small tacks, or paper clips should be picked up in advance so they don't get pulled into the vacuum cleaner, where they can damage or jam the appliance, causing costly repairs.

Turn the vacuum on, typically by a hand or foot switch, and then slowly push it back and forth over the area you're cleaning until you cover the whole area. Don't move too fast; give the machine time to do its job. If you move too fast, the suction will not pick up dirt properly.

Here's a dirty-but-true gross-out vacuum factoid: carpets can hold up to ten times their weight in dust and dirt. Eww!

For small areas where the vacuum doesn't fit, there is usually a caddy that carries accessories to clean in narrow spaces or small flat areas like stairs.

There are also handheld vacuums that are handy for cleaning up messes like your breakfast cornflakes or even your cornflakes with milk.

CHAPTER ELEVEN:
COOKING

Learning to prepare meals for yourself and others is an essential skill, assuming you like to eat. It's also a lot of fun, especially when you can make your favorite meals from scratch. As a bonus, you won't have to wait for your guardians to come home before you eat homemade food.

PREPARING THE BASICS BY YOURSELF

It's helpful to know how to prepare basic foods. Even if you don't yet know how to cook a whole meal, contributing small dishes is a helpful and enjoyable way to start. You might be excited to try out things you've seen your parents do in the kitchen, but don't be tempted to try anything without proper guidance and instruction. Start with basic cooking equipment like pots and pans before trying specialized equipment like crepe makers and fancy pressure cookers.

Wash your hands with soap and water before you touch any food items or utensils for meal preparation, and keep all food surfaces clean and sanitized. This prevents the spread of germs and keeps your food safe. Good kitchen hygiene is one of the most important habits to maintain.

When you're by yourself, only cook food that you know how to prepare. Don't try complex cooking techniques or brand-new recipes without an adult's permission.

When starting out, try cooking easy foods like scrambled eggs or French toast. Those foods are easy to prepare and satisfying to eat. There are excellent cookbooks available for beginning cooks, and the Internet is also a great place to find recipes for the young cook in the family.

USING KITCHEN UTENSILS SAFELY

"Handle with care" is good advice to heed when cooking and using the equipment and utensils in the kitchen. Abiding by these rules will reduce the chance of injury, keeping your cooking experience safe and enjoyable.

Be careful with sharp instruments. Utensils like knives, prongs, or anything with a blade should be used with care. If there are items that need to be cut or chopped, do so carefully, watching out for fingers.

Position pan handles away from you as a safety precaution; it's easier than you think to bump a panhandle and inadvertently dump hot soup, stew, or gravy on the floor or (heaven forbid) on yourself. Make a point to set pots and pans at angles that are out of the way while you work in the kitchen. The best position is for the handles to point towards the countertops rather than you or the hot burners. Pointing the handles over the burners could cause a burn if you try to lift the pot without a potholder to protect your hand.

Wash all utensils that are used with raw meat and fish products before using them for anything else. Raw meat and seafood can carry organisms that can cause humans to become ill, so be especially careful around these foods. This also includes your hands, spoons, ladles, knives, and chopping boards. Wipe the table surface, too. This will help curb the spread of germs and prevent the possibility of contamination and food poisoning.

Learn which utensils work best with different kitchen appliances in your household. For example, never put plastic bowls in the microwave, in the oven, or on the gas stove. Most plastic melts when exposed to heat, although some plastic is microwave safe. Metal and aluminum kitchenware should not be used in the microwave to avoid sparks and possible fire.

COOKING
SAFELY WITH HEAT

The stove, oven, and microwave are the major sources of heat used in cooking. Learn to use this equipment correctly with adults before using them on your own.

When cooking, don't stir food vigorously to avoid splatters on the stove or your arms and hands.

If you notice a rotten egg-like smell while cooking, turn off all heat sources and evacuate the kitchen. It could be a gas leak, in which case everyone should evacuate the house safely and call the gas company.

If a fire breaks out while cooking, do not attempt to put it out yourself. Call nearby adults to put it out using the fire extinguisher. For a serious fire or malfunction of the extinguisher, call the fire department. A metal lid can extinguish a fire in a frying pan, as can baking soda, although the latter option requires a **lot** of baking soda. It is important to **never pour water on any kind of oil fire** because it will cause the fire to spread and might even explode!

It is a really good idea to ask an adult to teach you how to use fire extinguishers by yourself as well as for help practicing how to put out different kinds of kitchen fires. This way, if a fire does catch, you are able to stay calm, know where the tools necessary to put the fire out are, and confidently can use them in an emergency. Hopefully, you will never have to use these skills in a real-life situation.

Always monitor the heat when using the stove while cooking. Monitoring it will prevent your food from burning.

CLEAN UP
AFTER YOURSELF

After all the fun you had cooking, you still have to clean up, one of the *most* important parts of cooking. (Who wants to walk into the kitchen first thing in the morning only to find a cold, greasy mess from last night's dinner?) Keeping the kitchen clean is one of the most important things to do every day. This includes properly putting food away to avoid unwanted guests, such as insects and bugs, wiping down all cooking and food preparation surfaces, and sweeping up crumbs.

If you follow a few commonsense rules, you'll enjoy cooking delicious food for years to come.

CHAPTER TWELVE:

DRESSING YOURSELF

Knowing what to wear and how to wear it can be a lot of fun and makes you feel good about yourself, too. It's also an essential part of your growing independence. You have likely been dressing yourself for years now, so you know something about dressing for the season and the occasion.

DRESSING FOR THE WEATHER

Dressing to suit the season and the weather forecast keeps you comfortable, healthy, and safe. In general, breathable fabrics are the most comfortable, and you can layer them for warmth or remove layers when you want to be cooler.

When the temperature is warm, choose lightweight fabrics that will be comfortable and help you stay cool. Consider materials such as jersey blends, cotton, and linen, which are comfortable and breathe easily. Synthetic fabrics such as acrylics don't breathe as well and tend to make you warm (which is great in winter). If you're not sure about a fabric, read the label inside the garment, which will tell you the fabric name and the percentage of content (i.e., 100% cotton).

Remember to wear light-colored fabrics which reflect light. Dark colors absorb light, as anyone will tell you who has ever worn a black T-shirt outdoors on a hot sunny day. A friend of mine wore a dark T-shirt to Disney World in Florida. He lived to tell about it but said it was a big mistake he would never repeat at an outdoor park on a sunny day. His day at the park in his black T-shirt was swelteringly hot since his black shirt absorbed the sun's rays and "baked him alive," to quote him directly.

During autumn and winter, when temperatures start going down, warmer clothing material made of wool, acrylic, flannel, and other synthetic fibers help retain heat and keep you warm. Layering garments also preserves warmth as air is trapped between layers, which insulates and retains your body heat, maintaining comfortable warmth. An example of layering clothing is a long-sleeved shirt under a long-sleeved sweater or cardigan. Another example of layering is a long-sleeved shirt, sweater vest, and blazer.

In seasons when the weather can be cool and warm on the same day, layering is ideal, as you can add or remove layers of clothing so you stay comfortable no matter what you have on.

MIX AND MATCH YOUR WARDROBE

One clever way to create multiple outfits is to buy clothing in complementary colors (for example: red, navy, black and gray) so you can make multiple shirt/pants/sweater outfits. The same goes for socks and shoes too. Navy and khaki also pair nicely, by the way. The possibilities are endless. This doesn't mean you can't enjoy other colors—just think of this mix-and-match idea as a wardrobe stretcher.

DRESS FOR
THE OCCASION

There are times in life when you need to know the right way to dress for certain events, holidays, or occasions. Examples are church services, dances, formal affairs, and costume parties (just to name a few).

Special clothing is often worn to show identity, like membership in a society, organization, or religion. One example is a uniform for boy scouts or girl scouts or a uniform for private schools. Many cultures have their own traditional forms of dress. Clothing is also a fun and creative way of showing your personality.

If you're not sure how to dress for a particular occasion, ask a trusted adult who will be able to give you guidance.

FORMAL SETTINGS

These are places and situations that require you to dress a certain way, often according to a stipulated dress code, to fit in or gain access. If you aren't sure what to wear, start with parents or other relatives, or call on school or church representatives, who will be glad to fill you in.

DRESSING FOR SCHOOL

Schools often have dress codes. If your school has a set of uniforms to be worn for the week, be sure they're clean and ready at the start of the week.

If there is no dress code, then you have more freedom as long as you adhere to the basic dress code. For example, many schools do not allow students to wear hats, sunglasses, or flip-flops in class.

Clothing items like jeans, shirts, and sweatshirts are great for a school outfit choice. Frequently you can find this information on your school or school district's website.

CHAPTER THIRTEEN:
NAVIGATION SKILLS

READING A MAP

A map is a representation of an area using diagrams or drawings. It covers all the physical features that can be identified within that area, like buildings, tourist attractions, neighborhoods, and bodies of water.

Reading a map is an essential skill that should be learned by kids. There are technological tools available now that can help with navigation, like GPS, Google Maps, or other navigation apps. These are extremely helpful, and it's a good idea to practice using them. But it's also smart to learn to read paper maps since not everyone owns a smartphone.

There are different types of maps, and they serve different purposes, but they all have one general goal: to guide you from one point to another. In general, a map is a diagram of an area, such as a country, state, or city. Roads, parks, and landmarks are shown, and you follow the map by locating your starting and ending points and keeping track of your progress as you travel, whether on foot, by car, or via public transportation.

There are road maps used by drivers, topographical maps used to go hiking and camping, tourist maps that show landmarks and sightseeing areas for tourists, and political maps that show demarcations between one country or county and another. Pick the one that suits your purpose. If you need to buy one, they are available in stores, gas stations, bookstores, and many other places. They are typically inexpensive.

To use the map, check its orientation; north should be at the top. North is a neutral orientation used to get your bearings and serves as a guide for other directions on the map.

After that is settled, study the map legend located on one side of the map. It contains symbols that can be interpreted to match the features of a particular environment. There are symbols for bodies of water (rivers, lakes, ponds, and lagoons), famous landmarks, areas within and outside towns and cities, mountains and valleys, and institutions like fire and police stations, schools, and points of interest such as stadiums or parks.

READING A COMPASS

A compass is a direction-finding tool that points out the cardinal directions (north, south, east, and west). A compass is a magnetic needle that always points north and rotates freely. When you hold the compass in your hand, it tells you the direction you're facing.

Planet Earth is a powerful magnet, and a compass is magnetic. A magnet has two poles, which are its primary centers of force, one at each end. The poles are connected by magnetic force lines. Because it aligns with the magnetic force lines of Earth, the compass needle points north.

A compass and a map are used to find directions to a place. The compass points you in the right direction, while the map shows the course to follow. Correctly using these tools will guide you to your chosen destination.

ASKING FOR DIRECTIONS

There will be times when you don't know where a certain building is or where a room is in a building. This could occur when you're in an unfamiliar town, visiting a college campus, or finding a hospital room to visit a friend. When this happens, learning how to ask for directions is a skill that comes in very handy.

There are ways to ask for directions and get the appropriate responses that will guide you down the right path.

Let's look at the ways **not** to ask for directions.

Think about what you need to say so you don't get tongue-tied. You may be hesitant, so try to keep your question short. Here are some examples: 1. "Can you help me find Room 100 in the Anderson Building?" 2. "Where is the public library?" 3. How do I get to 100 S. Main Street?

When going to an unfamiliar place, don't be tempted to go alone. It's easier and safer to ask for directions and figure out where to go that way.

Let's look at the best ways to get the answers you need from people.

Get straight to the point without overexplaining. If the person you talk to needs more information, they will ask you.

Be specific when asking for directions. It will help the other person understand what you want, and it will also clear up misconceptions.

There are also things to avoid when being given directions.

You might be frustrated or scared but stay calm. If you're in a public place, chances are the person you approach is frequently asked for help and is happy to help.

Don't interrupt the person helping you. Instead, listen to them talk. When they're done, you can then ask questions.

Avoid dark and lonely places. Always try to stay in areas that are well-lit and well-populated.

Asking for directions can prove to be a challenging task. However, it is important to learn it, as it will help in our day-to-day navigations.

CHAPTER FOURTEEN:
STUDY & RESEARCH SKILLS

As a student, you know that studying is a regular part of school life. You study to understand what's taught in class, unfamiliar concepts, and to pass tests.

Studying takes what you learn in school and commits it to memory.

- Improving study skills advances you to a higher level of learning, especially when you pay attention in class and listen attentively.

- Avoid distractions when you study. Listen to the teacher and don't distract others.

- Plan to read ahead for tests and quizzes. If a test is announced on Monday to be taken Friday afternoon, do you start studying Friday at lunch? No way! That's waiting until the eleventh hour. Break it down into steps, and study in manageable sessions from Monday to Thursday. On Friday afternoon, you'll be well-prepared to ace that test.

- Lay out a plan for schoolwork and real-life projects. Study time at home provides a more relaxed opportunity to learn outside of the classroom.

- Asking for help when something doesn't click makes studying easier. Your teacher will be glad to help resolve issues and answer your questions.

- Get a good night's sleep! Funny as it sounds, sleeping enhances the study process. The brain exerts itself when chunks of new information are added. Sleeping helps the brain rest and recover (your body, too). Sleep is very important for learning and for your overall health and well-being.

LEARN TO CHUNK

Chunking is a learning method used to simplify large pieces of information. It eliminates the fear of having to remember everything in your textbooks. Teachers use chunking to help students understand better by breaking down large topics for easier understanding and retention.

The key to chunking is mastering the art of finding patterns. The various forms of chunking are all fun ways of creating patterns. There are several ways to chunk.

The first method is to use acronyms. Acronyms are formed by the first letters of a group of words to help you remember. This is a proven method of memory retention. For example, in math class, you may hear the acronym "PEMDAS," which helps you remember the order of operations. PEMDAS stands for: <u>p</u>arentheses, <u>e</u>xponents, <u>m</u>ultiplication, <u>d</u>ivision, <u>a</u>ddition, and <u>s</u>ubtraction. Another is "SMART" goals: <u>s</u>pecific, <u>m</u>easurable, <u>a</u>ttainable, <u>r</u>elevant, and **time-bound**.

The second method is the use of acrostics, which uses the first letters of a set of words to make an easy-to-remember phrase. The following is an acrostic poem about summertime:

Sunshine warming my toes,

Underwater fun with my friends.
Making homemade ice cream on the porch,
Many long nights catching fireflies.
Early morning walks to the creek,
Reveling in the freedom of lazy days.

Generally, acronyms are better to use than acrostics because the latter needs to be decoded from the newly formed words to get the original meaning.

The third method groups similar concepts together. If there are items with associated links you need to remember, group them. They don't need the same spelling, pronunciation, or meaning. For example, pen and paper, book and pen, keyboard and mouse, bulb and switch.

Chunking works effectively by practicing what has already been learned. Repetition is the key here.

TAKING NOTES

Taking notes is probably not new to you. You already jot things down or put reminders in your phone when you come across something you really want to remember. When it comes to studying, take notes when you decide a speaker says something you want to remember and write it down in your own words to study later.

Note-taking enhances comprehension skills; as you listen, you learn, comprehend, and retain the knowledge you need to remember.

A great way to master taking notes is writing things down in a way you understand based on what the teacher says. Listen, comprehend, and then write down in your own words.

CREATE YOUR OWN STUDY SPACE

The spot you choose to study in really impacts learning. Tips for setting up an amazing study space are as follows:

- Look around the house for a spare table and chair.
- Always have good lighting.
- Get rid of all screens (you know what I mean).

Phones, tablets, and TV screens distract and hinder study time. You can't study in front of a TV; it will ruin your concentration (trust me on this).

Divide your time among the subjects you have to study, allotting more time to subjects that are more difficult. Use the Internet only for study purposes.

Accessing the Internet for information is a fine idea to broaden your knowledge about a subject.

However, do not be tempted to check messages or play games during study time.

BANISH NEGATIVE THINKING

If you're not following what you're studying, it's easy to start feeling lost or confused, which can lead to a down-in-the-dumps attitude. Let's face it: some subjects are more difficult than others, and the tough ones sometimes feel like a weight sitting on your shoulder.

If it starts getting you down, remind yourself that there are great help options to assist you. One is talking to your teacher. The teacher's job is to teach you in a way you can understand and remember. (Your teacher went into teaching because they *like* to teach; don't forget that. That's their job.) You might also consider an after-school session to clear up what you're having trouble with. Sometimes that's all it takes. Often, looking at the problem from a different angle makes all the difference, and suddenly the *aha!* light bulb goes off in your head. However, if you need more help, you can often find free tutors at your school, an older student who has already taken the class, or even a close relative who can explain it to you in a way that helps you understand better.

Negative thinking is bad no matter how you look at it, so look for solutions that get you past the bump in the road. Once that happens, you'll have a fresh perspective on learning that will give you fresh confidence.

CHAPTER FIFTEEN:
SELF-ENTERTAINMENT

Self-entertainment plays a vital role in helping young people develop creative skills. Filling up your own time makes you more self-aware of the activity, and you're accountable only to yourself. This boosts self-confidence.

USING TECHNOLOGY TO LEARN, PLAY, & ENTERTAIN

More than ever, technology impacts our daily lives. Common choices made by young people these days include texting friends, meeting new people on social media, and creating content for others to see and watch (YouTube, TikTok).

Besides using technology for recreational purposes, it can be used to access digital learning via tablets, laptops, and smartphones. Information is now accessible everywhere, no matter where and when you want it.

Let's look at ways technology can be used to build soft skills.

In some cases, technology helps the development of social skills. Lots of this usage is for communication, so it's a great way to practice interpersonal communication skills. Technology can be used in cooperation with other people when handled the right way. Another important social skill used throughout life is problem solving. To produce projects and collaborate on ideas in groups, learning to comfortably use technology is important now and will become increasingly important in the future.

Problem-solving skills can be developed using technology. The primary goal of video games can teach useful and transferrable problem-solving skills. When playing a game, you may wonder what will happen next or what could happen if a certain move is attempted. This serves as an exercise in problem solving.

Technology exposes you to things and ideas you might not see on an everyday basis. It makes you realize that life extends beyond the borders of the family and the classroom.

Talents can be discovered via interactive media. Technology offers opportunities to introduce activities you may partake in as adults, such as singing, learning to paint, and dancing lessons. Sports and trivia games fall into this category.

CREATING STEM CHALLENGES

STEM is an acronym for science, technology, engineering, and math. It's crucial today that children are equipped with the knowledge and abilities to solve problems, process information, and analyze evidence to make decisions in a constantly changing, more complicated environment.

STEM encourages problem solving, communication, and teamwork with others. Creating your own challenges can be a lot of fun and also provides planning, building, executing, and analytical skills.

A project to try at home is making a balloon parachute. You will need a balloon, string, and a small basket or another lightweight object to attach to it. It's fulfilling to watch your creation float into the sky, carried away by the wind. (See URL) https://www.youtube.com/watch?v=nTRQwJw UQkw

Using paper cups at home, you can build a tower by simply placing cups diagonally on each other to create spaces between them.

CHAPTER SIXTEEN:
WHAT TO DO ABOUT BULLIES

Bullying is an act of aggression and intimidation carried out by a person or group of people toward an individual or individuals. It occurs when the offender(s) think the victim can't or won't defend themself or won't report it to authorities who can make it stop.

Bullying happens verbally, online, and/or by physical force. Verbal bullying takes the form of offensive or hurtful language against a person and sometimes their family, ethnic background, religious community, or other features of their society.

Cyberbullying consists of threats or intimidation that take place virtually. Even though this type of bullying doesn't happen in person, it is just as serious and dangerous as if it did take place in person.

Physical bullying is any type of physical aggression that is applied to a victim as a form of intimidation without the victim's consent. It may take the form of fighting, shoving, sending an offensive or derogatory message, destruction of personal belongings, and more.

Bullying has been around for centuries, but in recent years it has been highly publicized and exposed as a form of aberrant delinquent behavior. Bullies pick on people whom they perceive as having less physical power or will to fight back. Some researchers suggest that bullies treat other kids the same way they themselves have been treated, perhaps from a direct bullying experience of their own. It can also stem from watching TV or movies that promote the bullying culture. Bullies seek notoriety from others to feel important and powerful.

WHAT CAN YOU CONTROL WHEN THINGS ARE OUT OF YOUR CONTROL

Bullying is a form of violence with a high degree of repetition if an opportunity arises. With proper assistance, it should be squashed immediately and *never* tolerated or ignored.

A peculiar aspect of bullying is that victims sometimes start to think *it's their fault.* Bullies manipulate emotions by playing a mind game of victim blaming.

Whenever possible, victims should stand their ground without fighting the aggressors. Instead, walk away, move to a quiet (and safe) place, and remain calm. File a report to the proper authorities as soon as possible.

Bullies tend to pick on quiet kids who are often alone. It helps to walk with a group of friends, staying close together. Bullies look for opportunities when victims are alone; they are much less interested in dealing with a group of people.

Don't act out in anger, which might entertain or encourage the bully. Clearly and forcefully tell them to stop, then walk away. This should not be perceived as running away or fear of fighting. It might hurt your pride to walk away, but it's the safest and best option. Move toward other people or go to a public place such as a school building right away.

If you have any evidence to prove you're being bullied, hold on to it. Show it to an adult or teacher who will help decide the best way to handle the situation.

Don't be silent; tell people what's happening to you. Tell your elder siblings, parents and friends, teachers, and other authorities so they can step in to handle the matter. Do not keep quiet! Bullies thrive in silence.

WHO TO TALK TO WHEN BEING BULLIED

Being bullied is painful, hard to endure, and its trauma can last a long time. If it continues, victims may suffer lower grades, depression, and anxiety. They may withdraw from normal activities, and their normal behavior may change.

It's hard to speak up after being treated in a deliberately hurtful manner, but if you keep it to yourself, it could drag on. Your silence emboldens the bully, who will continue to treat you miserably. That's why it's imperative to seek immediate help from adults who know how to handle such matters.

When you start letting people know about the untenable situation you've been put in, don't cover for the bully in any way by refusing to reveal their identity and the things they've done to you or made you do under threat of reprisal.

Tell a trusted adult about the situation, and identify the people responsible for it. An investigation will commence; you must be willing to provide information when needed, but you will have supportive adults around you.

WHAT TO DO WHEN SOMEONE YOU KNOW IS BEING BULLIED

Sometimes you can tell when a friend or classmate is being bullied. You may see it happen, or you may notice that someone just seems different than usual, perhaps more nervous or withdrawn. Encourage that friend to talk to a trusted adult as soon as possible.

Sometimes speaking up about bullying is difficult. The victim may worry that it will worsen after it's reported, or they'll be embarrassed or teased. These feelings are valid, so be gentle with victims of bullying. Try your best to let them know that the problem won't go away by ignoring it or hoping they can wait it out.

Remind your friend that there are punishments for bullies, and when the bully faces authorities and repercussions, it will stop. Victims of bullies may forget this or even fear it because they're so consumed by the trauma of it. Responsible authorities will intervene quickly when you tell them what's happening.

If you know bullying is taking place at school, encourage the victim to report it to a trusted adult. You can do it yourself if they agree, or you can offer to accompany them for moral support. It's important to understand that school officials are obligated to take such situations seriously, taking appropriate ameliorative steps without delay.

There is a common misconception that bullying helps people toughen up and become stronger. That's 100% wrong. Being the victim of bullying only makes people feel unsafe and insecure, and often they think less of themselves. Bullying is a form of violence that adults will put a stop to.

No one needs to be bullied into becoming stronger. It is not a rite of passage or something that makes you grow to be a stronger and better person. You become a strong, confident, self-assured individual by practicing good values, knowing your self-worth, and treating others with respect.

If you tend to treat others with disrespect, teasing them at every opportunity, know that it is also a form of bullying. Bullying (even teasing) other kids is not cool, no matter what people say or what you see in the media.

Do not engage in bullying, and never support those who do by saying nothing or standing by to watch. Do not keep quiet and ignore a victim of bullying when you can help. Be a good friend whenever you can.

SUMMARY

Life isn't always easy for kids and pre-teens as they face the challenging transition from childhood to the teenage years. It's tempting to assume that young people will pick up everything they need to know to survive and thrive, but that's not guaranteed.

Life Skills for Kids is a go-to guide to help young people learn essential skills needed to become responsible young adults. The book covers handling emotions, communication, and getting along with others. There are also how-to chapters about studying, writing a school paper, doing chores, dressing for any occasion, and basic cooking, so a kid doesn't go hungry after school.

This book was written to help young people transition smoothly to the next phase of life while providing fun activities to learn, as well as encouraging good study habits and responsible financial practices. They will learn how to interact responsibly with others in society and build excellent communication skills that will remain with them for life.

Bon voyage!

Made in United States
North Haven, CT
19 November 2022

26937131R00075